The Sport of Baseball

by Richard L. Hamm

SCHOOL PUBLISHERS

Cover, ©PhotoDisc; p.3, ©Joseph Sohm; ChromoSohm Inc./CORBIS; p.4–5, ©Rick Friedman/Corbis; p.6–7, ©Joseph Sohm; Visions of America/CORBIS; p.8, ©Digital Vision/PunchStock; p.9, ©Tim Shaffer/Reuters/Corbis; p.10, ©David Durochik/MLB Photos via Getty Images; p.11, ©RAY STUBBLEBINE/X00272/Reuters/Corbis; p.12, ©Mike Segar/Reuters/Corbis; p.13, ©CHARLES W. LUZIER/Reuters/Corbis; p.14, ©Anthony P. Bolante/Reuters/Corbis.

Copyright © by Harcourt, Inc.

All rights reserved. No part of this publication may be reproduced or transmitted in any form or by any means, electronic or mechanical, including photocopy, recording, or any information storage and retrieval system, without permission in writing from the publisher.

Requests for permission to make copies of any part of the work should be addressed to School Permissions and Copyrights, Harcourt, Inc., 6277 Sea Harbor Drive, Orlando, Florida 32887-6777. Fax: 407-345-2418.

HARCOURT and the Harcourt Logo are trademarks of Harcourt, Inc., registered in the United States of America and/or other jurisdictions.

Printed in China

ISBN 10: 0-15-350130-8
ISBN 13: 978-0-15-350130-2

Ordering Options
ISBN 10: 0-15-349939-7 (Grade 4 ELL Collection)
ISBN 13: 978-0-15-349939-5 (Grade 4 ELL Collection)
ISBN 10: 0-15-357272-8 (package of 5)
ISBN 13: 978-0-15-357272-2 (package of 5)

If you have received these materials as examination copies free of charge, Harcourt School Publishers retains title to the materials and they may not be resold. Resale of examination copies is strictly prohibited and is illegal.

Possession of this publication in print format does not entitle users to convert this publication, or any portion of it, into electronic format.

1 2 3 4 5 6 7 8 9 10 985 12 11 10 09 08 07 06

Baseball is a very popular sport. Many people in the United States play baseball. Baseball has been played in the United States since the early 1800s. Baseball is played in many other countries, such as Japan, Mexico, and Cuba.

Young children, teenagers, and adults play baseball. Both boys and girls play baseball. Millions of Americans go to a ballpark to watch a baseball game each year.

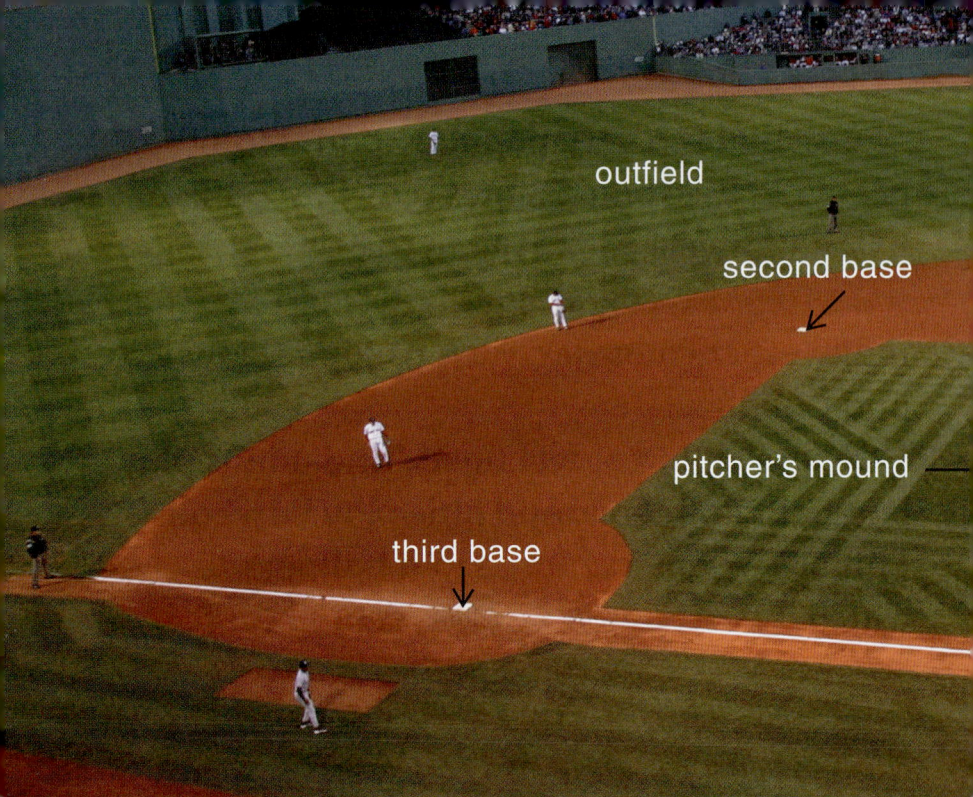

A baseball field is called a "diamond." That is because the field is shaped like a diamond. There are two main parts to a baseball field. One part is the infield. The other part is the outfield.

The infield has a home plate. This is where the batter stands when trying to hit the baseball. The pitcher throws the ball from the pitcher's mound.

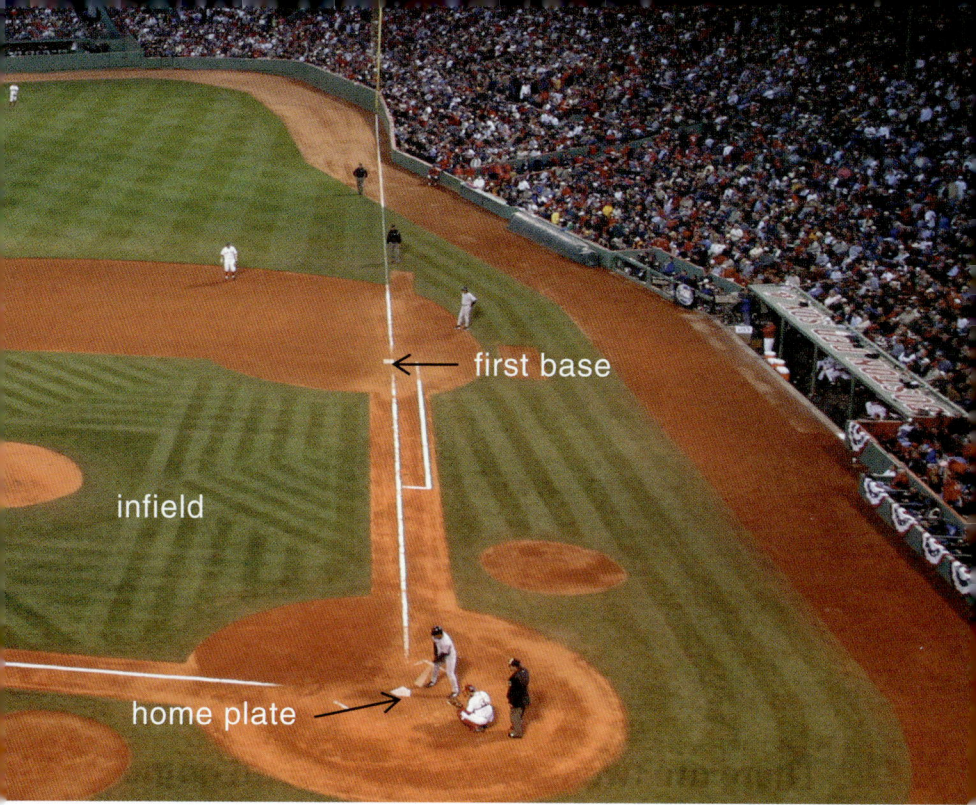

The infield also has three bases. They are called first, second, and third base. That is how baseball gets its name. The batter hits the ball and runs from one base to the next.

Home plate, the pitcher's mound, and the bases have dirt around them. The infield has grass in the middle.

The outfield is the area beyond the infield. The outfield is a large area that is covered with grass.

There are two teams in a baseball game. They take turns trying to score runs, or points. The team that scores the most runs wins. The game lasts for nine innings. Both teams have a chance to bat the ball during an inning. When one team makes three outs, the other team has a turn at bat. When a team is trying to score runs, it is "batting."

One player, the batter, goes to home plate to try to hit the ball. The other team's players stand in the field. They try to stop the batting team from scoring runs.

The pitcher throws the ball toward home plate. This throw is called a pitch. The batter tries to hit the ball with a bat. The ball can be difficult to hit because the pitcher throws it fast. The pitcher can also make the ball curve instead of just going straight. These curved pitches often make the batter swing the bat at the ball and miss.

A "strike" is when the batter swings at the ball but misses. It is also a strike if the ball goes right across home plate, and the batter does not swing. When a batter gets three strikes, the batter is "out."

If the pitcher does not throw the ball right across home plate, the pitch is called a "ball." After four balls, the batter gets a "walk" and goes to first base.

Let's say a player hits the ball a short distance and starts to run to first base. The players in the infield try to stop the ball, or to catch it. There is a player at first base, second base, and third base.

When the ball is hit a long way, an outfielder usually tries to catch it. There are three outfielders: left fielder, center fielder, and right fielder.

If the ball is hit into the air, and a fielder catches it before it hits the ground, the batter is out.

Sometimes the ball is hit into the outfield, and no one catches it. Then the batter runs to first base and stays there. If the batter hits the ball very hard, the batter might go to second base or even third base.

It is a home run if the ball is hit beyond the outfield. The batter gets to run all the way around the bases to home plate. A run is scored for the team!

Baseball players need equipment to play. They use mitts to protect their hands. A baseball is hard and can move very fast. The player's hands could get hurt without a mitt. Mitts also make it easier to catch the ball.

Players wear helmets when they bat. The helmets protect the players in case they are hit in the head by a pitch.

Players wear special shoes with sharp little spikes on the bottom. The spikes stop the player from slipping on the grass or dirt in the field.

Baseball players often practice catching baseballs. A coach will hit balls on the ground. That way, the players practice scooping the balls up. Also, the coach will hit balls into the air. That way the players can practice running to and catching fly balls.

Players also practice batting. They try to get better at swinging the bat to hit the ball. Pitchers practice pitching the ball. They learn to throw the ball fast and straight. Baseball players practice a lot to play the game better.

Baseball players also need to think. Sometimes baseball players have to decide whether to run to a base or stay on a base. Sometimes they have to decide where it would be best to throw the ball so that another player will be out.

Teamwork is also very important in baseball. Players work together so that they have the best possible team. Thinking, playing, and working together as a team are what make baseball so much fun!

Scaffolded Language Development

Concept Review Review with students what they learned about the game of baseball. Then play a game of word baseball. Each batter steps up to the plate and says a sentence about baseball. If the batter does so correctly, the batter advances to first base. Each time a batter says a sentence, the runners advance around the bases. When a runner reaches home plate, a run is scored. Batters may use the following sentence frames for their sentences, if necessary.

1. A _____ is used to play baseball.
2. _____ is part of a baseball field.
3. A _____ is a baseball player.

 ## Social Studies

Highlight a Map Find out whether there are any baseball teams in your state or in nearby states. Then provide students with an outline map of the United States. Point out your state and nearby states that have baseball teams. Have students write the names of the teams in each state.

 ### School-Home Connection

Draw a Picture Invite students to ask friends or family members about outdoor games that they enjoy. Then ask students to draw a picture of their family enjoying that game.

Word Count: 860(872)